DIVING
FOR
ADVENTURE

The author, Bob Marx, with about 300 pounds of silver coins in clumps.

DIVING
FOR
ADVENTURE

The Discovery of
the Golden Galleon *Maravilla*

Robert Marx

David McKay Company, Inc.
New York

Marx, Robert F. 1933-
Diving for adventure.

1. Maravilla (Ship) 2. Treasure-trove—Bahamas.
3. Underwater exploration. I. Title.
G530.M342M37   972.9'6   78-20617
ISBN 0-679-20454-7

10 9 8 7 6 5 4 3 2 1

Manufactured in the United States of America

To Henry Holmes
my good diving friend

Contents

Many women dive for adventure. Here, two divers inspect an iron cannon on the wreck of a British warship. One is holding a gold scabbard tip.

Why We Dive

Diving for sunken treasure is not a new profession; adventurous men and women have been risking their lives in deep water for thousands of years. Diving for treasure—or fame—is an exciting and rewarding life, especially if you are lucky enough to find a wrecked ship that contains gold and silver and jewels, or valuable historical artifacts.

If you are *not* lucky, diving can be one of the most frustrating jobs in the world—even more frustrating than punching a time clock twice a day, every working day of your life.

For years I was one of the most frustrated treasure hunters on the face of the earth. During a diving career of more than twenty years I had discovered and salvaged dozens of shipwrecks all over the globe, and I had earned a good reputation as an expert diver and an authority in the field of marine archaeology. I was envied by many

1

A Spanish treasure galleon, very similar to the **Maravilla.**

Hunting for "Marx's Phantom Wreck," a diver "flys" the "Pegassus," an underwater search vehicle.

time clock punchers who dreamed that they might some day dive for adventure—and come up rich. I enjoyed my life, and I was good at my job. Why was I frustrated?

During those twenty years I had been diving as a professional, I had found more than my share of treasure, but almost all of it had been claimed by one government or another, or had found its way into the pockets of the persons who had hired me to dive.

That is why I was frustrated, and that is why I dreamed.

Most divers, amateur or professional, dream of making a lucky "find"—the one find that will make them rich.

My dream was finding the *Maravilla*, the second richest Spanish treasure ship ever lost in the Western Hemisphere.

My dream was an old dream. For three years, between 1965 and 1968, I was excavating the sunken city of Port Royal, which had disappeared beneath the waters of Kingston Harbor during an earthquake in 1692. During those years, while working on the bottom, I dreamed that someday I would find the *Maravilla*, and the find would make me rich.

The *Maravilla* was *my* dream, but the wreck was real enough. Old Spanish records proved that, but few treasure hunters believed that the wreck would ever be found. Many of my friends in the treasure-hunting profession had made attempts to find the *Maravilla*, and some of them had begun to doubt that this 300-year old wreck really existed. They had begun to call it "Marx's Phantom Wreck."

Drawing of Spanish salvage divers at work on a shipwreck about the time of the loss of the Maravilla.

Divers holding gold coins found on a British warship located near the Maravilla. *Note the iron cannon at the left.*

1

The Treasure Fleets

The Spanish treasure ship *Nuestra Senora de la Maravilla* had been lost on Little Bahama Bank, a sandy reef forty miles from the Bahamas. The *Maravilla* went aground and broke up in shallow water on January 4, 1656 while sailing from the New World to Spain as part of a treasure fleet. The *Maravilla* was carrying gold and silver valued at $50,000,000 when she went down.

During the years that followed her loss, Spanish divers located and recovered a small portion of the *Maravilla* treasure, and during the Nineteenth Century several American salvage teams' tried—and failed—to find the wreck.

My obsession with finding the *Maravilla's* sunken treasure went back many years. It wasn't just the treasure I was after, but also proof that the wreck really existed and could be found.

A well-marked 72-pound silver bar off the wreck. The markings denote the fineness and weight of the silver, owner's initials, tally number of the bar, assayer's bite, and proof that taxes had been paid to the King of Spain.

I knew a great deal about the Spanish fleets, and I had researched the loss of the *Maravilla* in dusty archives in Spain. Spanish records from the Fifteenth and Sixteenth Centuries were amazingly complete.

The kings of Spain, like most rulers, were afraid of being cheated out of their treasures. They tried to stop smuggling by recording every bit of treasure that was shipped from the New World to Spain. Each piece of gold was stamped with its year of casting, its tally number, assayer's mark, total value in Spanish *reals,* weight, and owner's mark. The king's property was stamped with his coat of arms or his name. This information was recorded. Many of those records still exist. Every chest of coins or precious stones was sealed by a royal official, and the value of the contents was stamped on the outside. The records went into a registry on the ship that would carry it to Spain, and there were three copies of each register. One was placed aboard the *capitana* of the *flota,* the second aboard the *almiranta,* and the third was kept at the port of embarkation until the following year, when it was checked against the original and the other two copies. Spanish kings didn't take any chances with their gold. If they lost anything, they wanted to be sure it was to storms, or pirates, or the hated British.

But let's go back a century before the loss of the *Maravilla* and look at the importance of the New World treasures to Europe. The *Maravilla* was just one of thousands of galleons that had sailed to America during the three centuries the Spanish controlled the New World, and only one of many that were lost. But she was

Author's daughter, Hilary, with a 70-pound silver bar. She has been a scuba diver since she was five years old.

10

*Two Spanish pieces of eight. The corrosion has been
removed from the coin on the right in an electrolytic bath.*

of special importance because she was the richest galleon lost up to that time and she sank with treasure that was vital to Spain, which was on the edge of bankruptcy.

The Spaniards, greedy for the New World's precious metals, were cruel taskmasters, and over the years thousands of Indian slaves perished from overwork. Later, after the surface veins were exhausted and deep shafts had to be dug, cave-ins and poor ventilation took a further toll of Indian laborers and black African slaves.

Each year more treasure was carried from the New World to Spain. In 1508 the return of a single ship carrying gold and pearls worth 50,000 *pesos* (pieces of eight) was cause for rejoicing in Spain. By 1523 a single ship carried as much as 400,000 *pesos,* and in 1535 four ships brought 2,500,000 *pesos* from Peru. After the big mines got into full swing, the amount of treasure pouring into Spain soared, and in 1587 more than 16,000,000 *pesos* were transported from Mexico alone. Only a small portion of the wealth of the New World came from gold, for gold was expensive to mine. The real wealth was in silver, and so much silver was mined and put into circulation that its value dropped to a fifteenth of the value of gold.

When trade with the Spanish colonies began, the ships crossing the Atlantic were very small. Most were less than a hundred tons and measured fifty to fifty-five feet from stem to stern and eighteen feet across the beam.* These ships, known as caravels, had been developed early in the Fifteenth Century by the Portuguese for voyages of exploration, and the Spaniards found them well suited for Transatlantic voyages. Caravels carried

*Some did not exceed fifty tons and measured only thirty-five to fifty feet in length and fifteen feet across the beam.

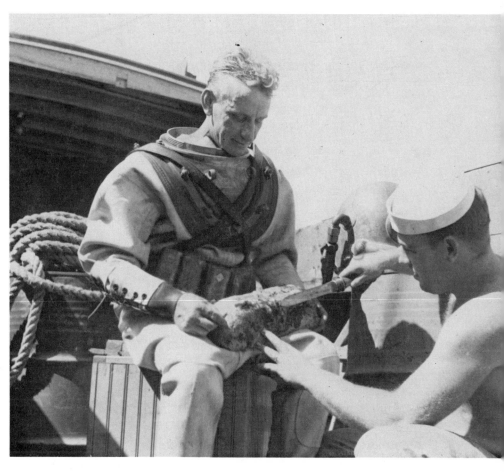

Diver Art McKee, wearing a diving suit, holds a silver bar he recovered off a salvaged Spanish ship.

two or three masts with lateen sails and were able to sail close to the wind and to make good speed. However, their small size soon made the little caravels obsolete for the growing Transatlantic trade. Bigger ships were needed, so bigger ships were built.

The credit for designing the ship that was to be used in Transatlantic navigation for more than 250 years belongs to Don Alvaro de Bazan, Spain's most illustrious naval commander during the Sixteenth Century. He first wanted to adapt galleys for the long ocean crossing, but too much cargo space was taken up by food and water for the rowers. He then devised a large vessel of several hundreds tons, built on long, straight lines, with two or three decks, three or four masts, and a spread of square sails. These galleons were top-heavy and always in danger of capsizing in a storm but they had the space and speed that were necessary for the Transatlantic trade. By the early 1550s galleons averaging between three hundred and five hundred tons were handling the bulk of the commerce with the colonies.

In 1526 a law was passed that specified that all Spanish merchant ships sailing to and from the American colonies had to be armed and had to sail in groups of no fewer than ten. Although an occasional lone ship was permitted to make the voyage, it had to have a special license and could not carry valuable cargo. The majority of the ships sailed in the organized *flotas*. By the middle of the century, galleons had superceded all other cargo ships on the Transatlantic run, although smaller pinks, flyboats, tartans, sloops, and pinnaces also sailed with the *flotas*.

The ships in the *flota* and their cargoes were usually defended by two heavily-armed galleons. One was the *capitana,* which was commanded by the Captain General of the *flota.* If Spain was at war with another country, or if they expected to be attacked by pirates, the number of heavily-armed galleons was increased. "Heavily-armed" meant just that. All the ships were armed. A merchant galleon of 400 tons might carry ten or twelve cannon, but a war galleon might carry as many as fifty, arranged in two or three tiers. The largest Spanish cannon was the *demiculverins,* which weighed two tons and fired a ball of seven to twelve pounds. It had a range of a thousand paces, point-blank, and more than twice that distance in trajectory. The cannon were generally made of brass. Iron was used only when brass was in short supply, for iron cannon heated quickly and sometimes exploded after repeated firing, killing more Spanish gunners than the enemy.

The Spaniards needed their guns. Smuggling presented a real danger to the Spanish Crown, but *freebooters* were a greater danger. Pirates roamed the high seas, eager to steal Spain's treasures from her colonies. (In the sixteenth century, as more and more treasure was carried to Spain, the ranks of the pirates swelled.) Among the most troublesome were English *Sea Dogs* such as John Hawkins and Francis Drake, who attacked Spanish shipping and settlements with impudence. King Phillip II, the ruler of Spain from 1556 to 1598, accused the British Ruler, Queen Elizabeth, of trying to steal his territories in America. This Elizabeth denied repeatedly. No nation was strong enough to risk

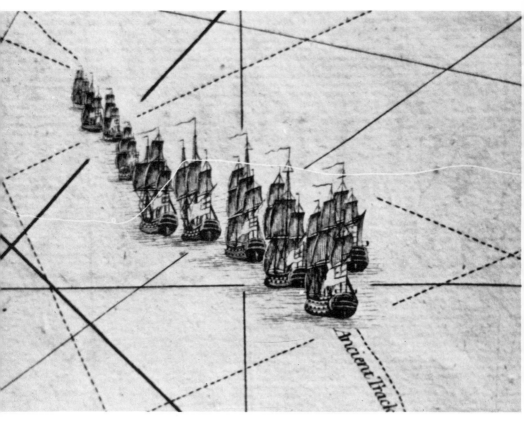

A Spanish treasure fleet under sail.

Years after the **Maravilla** *went down, diver John Hollister cleans the growth off one of her many bronze cannon.*

an open challenge to Spain's power, but British ships continued to raid the *flotas*.

The *flota* system was Spain's lifeline. The vast riches of America kept the Spanish economy afloat, and any interruption in the delivery of treasure threatened the prosperity of the nation, from the Crown, whose share of the treasure was usually mortgaged to foreign bankers, down to the man in the street, waiting for his wages.

Beginning in 1592, three *flotas* were sailing to the American colonies each year. The New Spain and Tierra Firme *flotas* maintained their usual schedules, carrying cargoes of lumber, indigo and sugar. Each of eight to twelve galleons carried a company of two hundred soldiers and much artillery. A third *flota*, The Galleons, was sometimes called "the treasure fleet." It carried no cargo to the American colonies, but sailed for only one purpose—to bring back treasure.

More wealth poured into Spain from her overseas empire between 1590 and 1600 than in any previous decade. It was truly the Golden Decade of the Golden Age.

The Dutch, English, and French established settlements in the Caribbean and these presented a grave threat to Spain's safe transportation of American treasure. The increased danger from enemy ships was just another of many problems faced by the *flotas*. By 1648 less and less treasure was crossing the Atlantic, and large convoys of ships were no longer required. The intervals between voyages became longer and longer, and there was sometimes a gap of four or five years between the departure of one *flota* and the next. *Flotas* sometimes waited years to return home rather than face combat with lurking enemy fleets.

Two of the 11-foot bronze cannon off the wreck.

*Treasure that never reached Spain: a four-pound gold disc,
gold coins, emeralds, and other gemstones. ·*

My dream ship, the *Maravilla,* sailed in a fleet of 22 ships. The *Maravilla* had just had her rudder and mizzenmast replaced. Shortages of food had caused a long delay in port, and seamen had deserted in New World ports that had been visited by the fleet, and they had been replaced by prisoners from Havana's prison. Eight other merchantmen had joined the Spanish fleet in Cuba. Eight galleons were capable of carrying the treasure, but it was decided to carry most of it aboard the *Capitana* and the *Maravilla.* Each of these two galleons carried more than five million pesos in treasure—gold, silver, jewelry, precious stones, and pearls.

The *Maravilla* had the added honor of carrying a solid gold statue of the Madonna and Child.

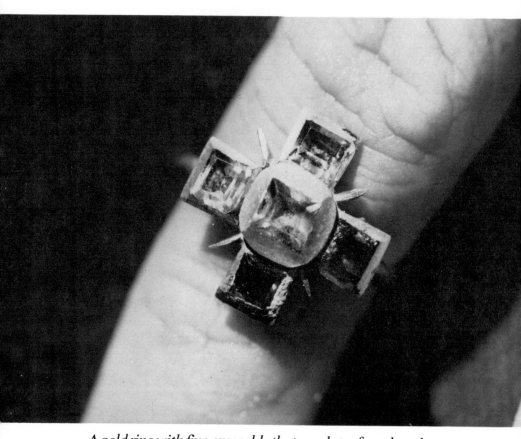

A gold ring with five emeralds that was later found on the Maravilla.

2

The Loss of the Maravilla

The fleet set sail in perfect weather under a blazing noon sun on January 1, 1656. According to Don Diego Portichuelo de Ribandeneyra, who had headed the Holy Inquisition in Lima for many years and was then sailing as a passenger on the *Maravilla*, many of the *Maravilla's* passengers had succumbed to a fever in Havana and were sick when they left the port. Seven persons died the first day out and six more the second. Then, around midnight on January 4, a lookout on the *Maravilla*, which was the lead ship in the fleet, discovered the ship was in shallow water on a sand bank. A cannon was fired to warn the other ships. In the confusion that followed several ships continued on their original headings, while others pointed their bows west toward deep water. The galleon

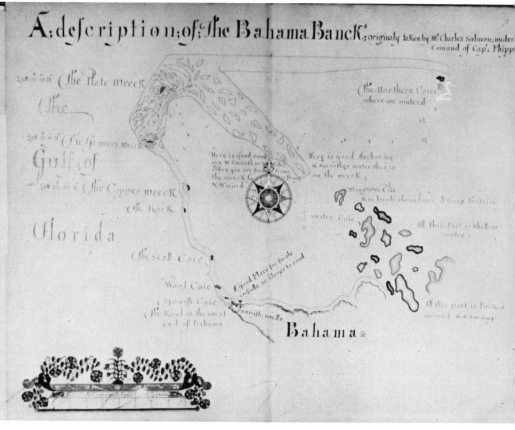

A chart made in 1683 by William Phipps, who salvaged some of the treasure off the Maravilla. "The Plate Wreck" *denotes the* Maravilla.

Jesus Maria was the first to get into trouble. She struck a coral head and lost her rudder, and then anchored in four fathoms of water.

There was panic aboard the *Maravilla*. Everyone rushed topside in fear for their lives. Some thought they had been attacked by enemy ships. The *Maravilla* had changed course and was trying to sail off the bank but the *Capitana,* the last ship in the formation, continued north and collided with the *Maravilla*. Both galleons were locked together. Their crews chopped at the rigging to separate them. The *Capitana* continued on its voyage, expecting the *Maravilla* to follow. But the *Maravilla* had a large hole in her bow below the waterline, and began to fill with water. Four of the ship's pumps were manned and even the passengers were bailing, but there was no chance of saving the ship. It was decided to run her aground to save their lives and the treasure. A strong current pushed the galleon east into shallower water as the rest of the fleet disappeared in the dark. Half an hour later the galleon struck violently on a coral reef and sank on a sandy bottom in thirty feet of water. Her fore and stern castles remained out of the water. As the ship settled to the bottom, a strong northerly wind began to blow, churning up waves that soon began to dash the ship to pieces. The crew and passengers fought for places in the vessel's two longboats or drifted away on debris, never to be seen again. Some clung to pieces of the galleon that still remained above the water. Then the ship broke in two. The bow, which was filled with water, remained in the same place, but the bouyant main section of the hull was lifted by the high seas and was carried away.

After centuries on the Little Bahama Bank, a fragment of the
Maravilla's *wooden keel is raised to the surface.*

Working on Little Bahama Bank, divers use an airlift, which works on the principle of a vacuum cleaner, to remove sand in their search for the wreck.

By sunrise there were only 45 survivors clinging to the wreck. They could see the *Jesus Maria* anchored to the north, but were unable to attract her attention. The crew of the *Jesus Maria* finally sighted the remains of the *Maravilla* and sent a long boat to rescue the survivors. The wind, currents, and seas were so bad that the boat returned to the ship. When the wind dropped they made another attempt. Some survivors jumped overboard and tried to swim to the boat but only three reached it safely. It took the rescue boat four hours to fight its way back to the *Jesus Maria*. The remaining survivors were picked up later and taken to the *Jesus Maria*. By late afternoon waves had destroyed the bow section and nothing could then be seen of the wreck of the *Maravilla*. Several days later, when the storm abated, the pilot of the *Jesus Maria* placed buoys over the wreck. The *Jesus Maria* was towed off the shallow bank and started after the fleet. Near the Bermuda Islands the *Jesus Maria* was badly damaged in another storm and the ship was sailed to Puerto Rico for repairs.

The Spanish fleet sailed under shortened sail for three days, hoping that the *Maravilla* and *Jesus Maria* would rejoin them. Six weeks later, as the fleet approached Spain, it was attacked by Barbary pirates and two of the merchantmen were captured. The others safely entered port, where the king seized what was left of the treasure.

When the galleon *Jesus Maria* reached Cartagena, the governor heard of the *Maravilla's* loss. He immediately initiated action to salvage the wreck. Six small

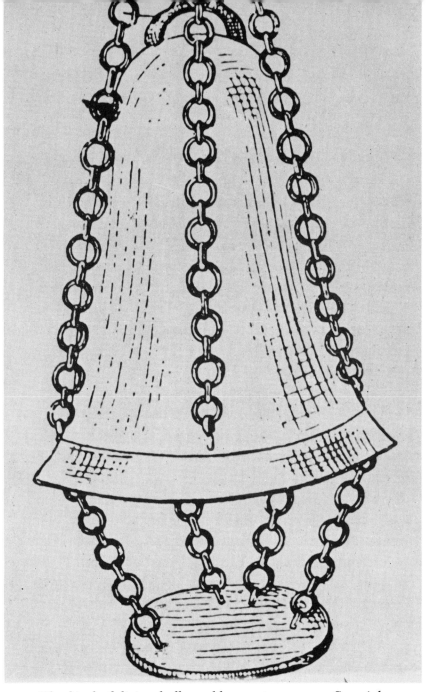

The kind of diving bell used by contemporary Spanish salvage divers.

ships were selected as salvage vessels. Each carried two large lead diving bells, soldiers, divers, and seamen to sail the vessels.

The six ships sailed from Cartagena on April 27, 1656, but they couldn't find the wreck when they reached the Little Bahama Bank. For six days they dragged cables over the bank and then they found the bow section of the wreck. They didn't find the main section, which contained most of the treasure, including the Madonna and Child. During the first day of diving the Spaniards recovered 174 silver bars, 34,000 silver *pesos*, two chests of gold coins and bars, four chests of precious stones and pearls, and seven chests of silver objects. By the end of the thirteenth day they had brought up 480,000 *pesos* in treasure, plus 12 small bronze cannon.

More divers worked at the site that summer and they brought up more than 650,000 *pesos* in treasure and four more bronze cannon from the bow section of the wreck. The Spaniards returned to the wreck many times, but the divers found little except for a few ballast stones. More treasure was found in 1677 and then in October, 1680 a hurricane struck the Caribbean and passed over the Little Bahama Bank and uncovered part of the wreck. A small fishing vessel from Boston "fished up" seven silver bars and a barrel full of silver coins. Then, time and shifting sands hid the *Maravilla* again.

I found the *Maravilla*—the "Phantom Wreck"—on August 24, 1972. Five of us were aboard our salvage vessel, the *Grifon,* a 72-foot converted shrimp boat.

Two divers inspecting an old anchor found during the search for the Maravilla.

The 76-foot salvage vessel Grifon *used to locate and salvage the* Maravilla. *Note the "blaster" on the stern.*

3

Diving for Adventure

At the time she was the largest and best-equipped vessel in the treasure hunting business. Her 9,000 gallons of fuel enabled her to stay at sea for months. She carried three radios, a radio directional-finder, two fathometers, radar, a good LORAN set for precision positioning, side-scanning sonar, and a magnetometer. The magnetometer was our main search instrument. Invented during World War II to detect enemy submarines, treasure hunters use it to find concentrations of metal on the ocean floor.

The main excavation tool on the *Grifon* was the "blaster," which was also called the "blower" or "mailbox." It was a steel tube that used the boat's propeller wash to throw a stream of water against the bottom, blasting away the mud and sand that may hide a hidden treasure.

When using the blaster the *Grifon* was kept stationary by four anchors—two off the bow and two off the

Bob Marx preparing the sensor head of a magnetometer.

stern. They took the greatest strain when the blaster was in action. I have seen a six-pound cannon ball blasted more than fifty feet when a blaster was run too fast. the blaster on the *Grifon* was so powerful it could be used to remove heavy ballast stones from a wreck. Divers on the bottom enjoy good visibility because the propeller sucks in clear surface water and pushes it to the bottom.

By August, 1972, when we finally located the wreck of the *Maravilla*, we had been searching for three months. Our skipper was convinced that anyone who searches for treasure must be crazy and that fishing offered better opportunities. But he wasn't immune to the lure of sunken treasure and he underwent a complete transformation when we finally found the wreck. His eyes burned with excitement and he came down with a raging case of "treasure fever" when the first treasure was brought aboard.

We were ready to give up when we finally found the *Maravilla*. We had searched fifty square miles with negative results. I reminded the crew that we would have wasted $100,000 of our financial backer's money if we went home. We decided to spend one more week searching for the wreck. That was on August 19. I stayed up most of that night going over charts and my notes, trying to figure out why we had failed to find the *Maravilla*, but the next day again produced nothing. When it was too dark to search any longer, we returned to the *Grifon* and I was asked: "Did you get enough exercise? We ought to have *something* to show for the waste of time and money."

Diver using an underwater metal detector on a wreck site.

A better view of the "blaster" on the Grifon.

We enlarged the search area during the next three days and we got repeats on targets we had found earlier in the summer. Each day the tension aboard the vessel mounted. We had found a piece of modern pipe on the bottom and the captain asked: "Are you sure there's nothing *under* that iron pipe?"

"Leave the treasure hunting to us," one of the divers told him.

Tempers were getting short. But I agreed with the captain, and we repositioned the boat over the spot and lowered the blaster.

One diver was on the bottom, watching the large hole in the making. When the hole was twenty feet deep, he surfaced and announced that he saw nothing. I ordered him to go back down, but some of the crew wanted to head for port. I challenged this, but I lost the argument and two of us jumped into the skiff to retrieve the stern anchors.

To our great surprise, two Spanish-type ballast stones were wedged between the flukes of one of the anchors!

"What if the *Maravilla* is down there and we miss it after all these months of hard work?" one diver asked, as we headed toward the Florida coast. It took four days of constant nagging for my wife to get me to go back to the treasure site—"just once more." And it took a great deal of talking to get other divers to go back with me. Some were convinced we were wasting our time, but we returned once more to the spot where the ballast stones had been found. We only carried enough food and fuel for two days.

Dick Anderson holds a beautiful piece of a gold belt.

The sun was climbing the eastern horizon when we found the bright red buoy I had left to mark the spot.

Playful bottle-nosed dolphins were cavorting around the vessel as we prepared to dive. When I went in, one dolphin came up and rubbed his back across my legs, a sign of welcome. I grabbed his dorsal fin and rode him under the water.

Looking down through the blue-green water I saw a beautiful coral reef. I jack-knifed and headed for the reef, swimming through a school of red snappers. Then I saw that the reef was covered with scattered ballast stones, ceramic sherds, and small pieces of coral-encrusted iron objects. I grabbed a handful of ceramic sherds and rushed back to the *Grifon*, beaming with excitement. Ceramic storage containers were used to carry water and wine aboard Spanish ships.

One of our crew said: "What's that junk?" He wanted to go back to port!

We repositioned the *Grifon* and went down again. I followed a large grouper fish to a small cave. Sticking my head inside, I spotted an olive jar and a large copper kettle. I grabbed both objects and struggled to the surface. Bad weather was coming, but I was too excited to care. I dove to the bottom again. That time I found a clay smoking pipe, which I took back to the *Grifon*. I compared it with hundreds of others in a book I always carried for dating purposes. The one I had found dated between 1680 and 1700—years after the *Maravilla* had been lost!

"Do we head for Florida now?" someone asked, but I was still sure we were on to a good thing.

Anderson drinking from a silver pitcher he recovered.

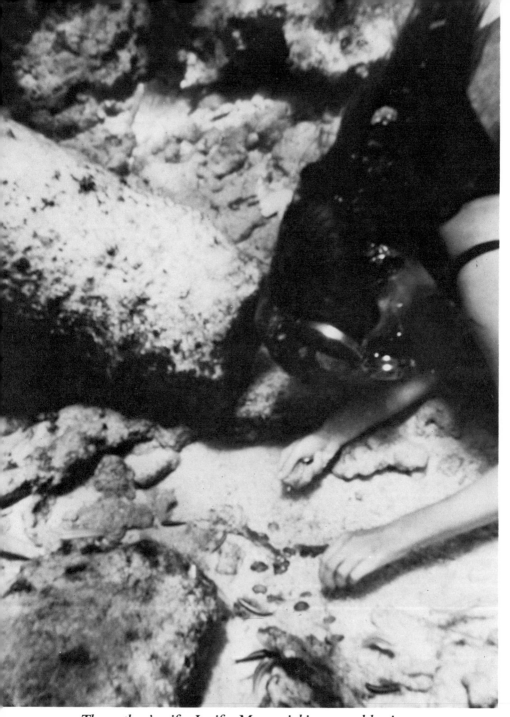

*The author's wife, Jenifer Marx, picking up gold coins next to
a coral-encrusted iron cannon.*

Two of us went back down together. We dug through six feet of sand and reached the limestone bottom. It was covered with ballast stones and more olive jar sherds. Four hours and a dozen holes later, I began to get discouraged. We had uncovered an area about the size of a tennis court and had little to show for it. We moved the *Grifon* 200 feet north from the reef and dug a new series of test holes. The first hole produced a beautiful jade axe head, more olive sherds, and some ballast stones. When I surfaced with the axe head, the *Black Beard,* a vessel belonging to a rival treasure group, was anchored nearby. Two of their crew were armed with guns! I asked them what they wanted.

"Just a friendly chat," one replied, so I agreed to swim over and talk with them.

"Marx, you really *are* crazy," our captain said. "If they want a bunch of ballast stones and pottery, let them have it. You'll get us all killed."

The crew of the *Black Beard* wanted to fight, not talk, and it took me two hours to convince them we were excavating a U.S. Civil War blockade runner. They finally steamed off towards the north and I went back to the *Grifon.* It was almost dark, but I knew I would have a sleepless night if I didn't dive again. I *knew* we were anchored over the *Maravilla.*

Several new holes produced more ballast stones and ceramic sherds, and it was difficult to see on the bottom. We decided to blast just one more hole. It took the blaster ten minutes to blow away ten feet of sand, digging a hole twenty feet in diameter. Groping around in the dark, I found a large silver tray and then two silver spoons. My

A diver plays with the dolphins that often frolicked around the
Maravilla *wreck site.*

44

Dave Edgell holding a large grouper and barracuda that he had speared for dinner.

Silver bars, coral-encrusted pieces of eight, and a sword on the right, that were later found on the wreck.

partner took them up to the *Grifon*. I was groping in total darkness when I found a strange shape, which I carried to the surface. I held it up to the lights that the captain had hung over the stern. I had found a golden dish with two silver spoons, a silver fork, a silver ink well, a silver snuff box, two pairs of brass navigational dividers, and a brass ruler. I dropped them on deck and dove again. I had to find something that would date and identify the wreck. I wasn't going to let the darkness stop me now. I shifted ballast stones and ceramic sherds from side to side, hoping for a miracle. Then I found it—a Spanish coin, a piece of eight. I blasted for the surface like a missile. I was too exhausted to move, so I asked someone to bring me half a lemon. The coin had a coating of silver sulfide that concealed its markings. I rubbed the lemon gently over the coin and the black coating began to disappear. Suddenly the date on the coin appeared—1655. We had found the *Maravilla*!

Divers, Dave Edgell, left, and Mike Daniel, with 300 pounds of silver coins in clumps.

48

4

A Fortune in Treasure

During the days, weeks, and months that followed, we brought a fortune to the surface. We found gold and silver bars, thousands of gold and silver coins, emeralds and diamonds, a golden chain, beautiful Chinese porcelain, and thousands of pounds of iron and brass artifacts. And during those months, while we labored on the bottom with the water-jet blaster, we were buffeted by high winds and rough seas and water spouts, and we were threatened by sharks, treasure pirates, and the crews of rival salvage boats. The men were as dangerous as the sharks. There were days when we had to chase both sharks and pirates away by firing into the water with rifles and a submachine gun, and once we attempted to ram a rival boat when it refused to leave the treasure site.

We worked long and hard, and at times we overloaded the "goodie bag," the container we used to hoist the treasure to the boat on the surface. More than once the line broke and silver bars rained down around our heads.

Diver inspects the jaws of a 14-foot tiger shark that had to be killed on the wreck site.

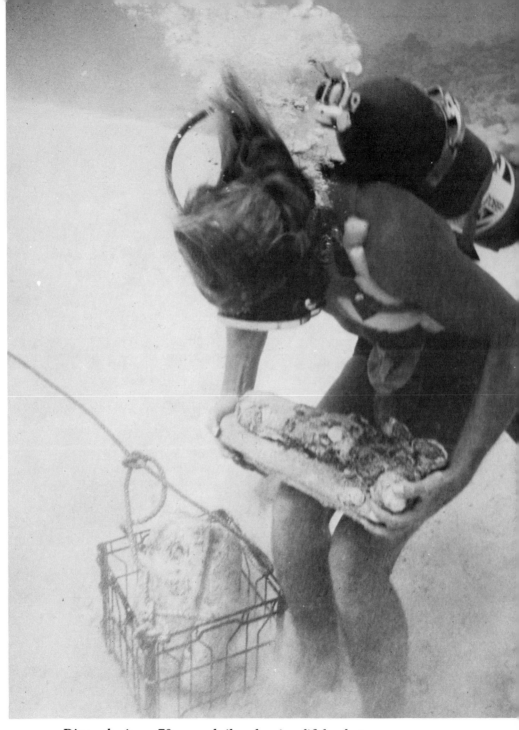

Diver placing a 70-pound silver bar in a lift basket.

During happier times, Edgell holds a gold coin next to three large silver bars. Note the diver at work in a hole in background.

We hoisted a king's ransom to the surface, and we had scarcely begun to work the "find." I was sure that my luck had turned, and the *Maravilla* treasure would make me rich.

Did it happen? Well, no—but it wasn't sharks or bad weather that finally cheated me out of my Spanish fortune. In the end, as has happened to me too many times in the past, it was the "pirates"—both ashore and at sea—who made it impossible to finish our work at the wreck of the *Nuestra Senora de la Maravilla*. Although the treasure site was in international waters, they tied us up with legal red tape, and other treasure hunters moved in and destroyed the reef, making it harder and harder to locate the bones of the galleon. On one of our most discouraging days we found nothing except more ballast stones—and a 20th Century beer bottle.

"Quit," my wife told me. "Forget the *Maravilla*; forget treasure hunting! All it's ever brought you is trouble!"

In the end I decided that she was right. I was tempted at times to team up with one of the "pirate" outfits, but I couldn't risk my reputation as an underwater archaeologist, so I turned my back on the *Maravilla*.

Much of the *Maravilla's* treasure, including the solid gold statue of the Madonna and Child, is still out there, waiting to be recovered.

I know where it lies. I may have to wait for years, but I feel confident, that some day I'll return to the Little Bahama Bank and I'll recover the millions of dollars in treasure that still rests in the main section of the Golden Galleon *Maravilla*.

Maybe that's what diving for adventure is all about.

Riding a 10-foot hammerhead shark above a wreck site is part of the fun of diving for adventure.

54

Glossary

ALMIRANTA—Heavily armed galleon commanded by an admiral.

ARCHIVES—Place where public records and documents are kept.

ARTIFACTS—Objects made or fashioned by man.

ASSAYER'S MARK—Initials on Spanish bullion of assayer who tested metal's purity.

BALLAST STONES—Stones carried in a ship's hold to give stability.

BANK—A shallow place or shoal in the sea.

BEAM—The breadth of a ship at its widest.

BLOCKADE RUNNER—A ship that attempts to sail into a blockaded port.

BOW—Forward part of a vessel.

CAPITANA—Flagship commanded by the captain general: heavily armed.

CARAVEL—Small, swift, narrow ship with lateen sails.

CARTAGENA—Caribbean seaport in Colombia.

CASTING—Pouring molten metal into molds, such as bars.

CERAMIC SHERDS—Fragments of pottery.

CORAL HEAD—A large coral formation rising above the surrounding ocean bottom.

FLOTA—A convoy of galleons and smaller, faster ships.

FLYBOAT—Dutch designed flat-bottomed sailing vessel: small and fast.

FREEBOOTER—A pirate or buccaneer.

GALLEON—Large Spanish ship with one or more decks at the bow and three or four at the stern.

GALLEY—Long, low ship propelled by sail and oar.

HOLY INQUISITION—A Roman Catholic tribunal that searched for and punished nonbelievers.

INDIGO—A blue dye obtained from the indigo shrub: one of the New World's chief exports.

LATEEN—A triangular sail.

LONGBOAT—The largest boat carried on a sailing ship.

LORAN—Position locating system utilizing radio signals.

NEW WORLD—Western Hemisphere.

OWNER'S MARK—Initials on a piece of Spanish bullion identifying the owner.

PESO—A Spanish silver coin worth eight reals.

PIECE OF EIGHT—A Spanish silver coin, worth eight reals.

PILOT—The man responsible for directing the course of a ship.

PINK—Small, swift ship with a narrow stern.

PINNACE—Small swift sailing vessel.

PORT OF EMBARKATION—Port from which a ship sails.

REAL—A former Spanish monetary unit and silver coin issued in denominations of eight, four, two, one.

REEF—A ridge of coral, rock, or sand near the water's surface.

SLOOP—A fore-and-aft rigged boat, usually with two sails.

SONAR—Object-locating apparatus using high frequency sound waves.

STEM TO STERN—From one end of a ship to the other.

STERN CASTLE—A small castle-like structure on the rear of a ship.

TALLY NUMBER—Identification number marked on Spanish bullion.

TARTAN—Small single-masted Mediterranean ship with a large lateen sail.